31 DAYS OF SINGLE. ON PURPOSE.

ALSO BY JOHN KIM

I Used to Be a Miserable F*ck

Single. On Purpose.

It's Not Me, It's You (with Vanessa Bennett)

31 DAYS OF SINGLE. ON PURPOSE.

REDEFINE EVERYTHING. FIND YOURSELF FIRST.

JOHN KIM

 HarperOne

An Imprint of HarperCollins*Publishers*

HarperCollins books may be purchased for educational, business, or sales promotional use. For information, please email the Special Markets Department at SPsales@harpercollins.com.

FIRST EDITION

All art courtesy of Shutterstock, except author photograph on page 97, which is courtesy of the author.

Library of Congress Cataloging-in-Publication Data is available upon request.

ISBN 978-0-06-330365-2

23 24 25 CPI 10 9 8 7 6 5 4 3 2

31 DAYS OF SINGLE.
ON
PURPOSE.

INTRODUCTION

The greatest moments of growth and evolution happen when you're single.

How do I know? I've been a therapist for twelve years, and I've spent long stretches of my life being single myself. Let's be clear—being single is *not* when you're in the final stages of a relationship that went sour and you're still recovering from the wreck. It's not when you're having Tinder conversations with eight different people and you're in varying stages of leading them all on. It's not when your mind is clouded with the dopamine that comes with meeting someone new. You will know when you are truly and absolutely *single*. In the grandest sense of the word. It's when you're alone and free and don't have to answer to anyone but yourself. When you're not sharing your Google calendar with anyone. When days are wide and passion is something you can actually ride. That's when the growth soil is the richest. And if that sounds like you, then that time is now.

This book is about recognizing that being single is not to be taken lightly. It is not the empty time between relationships. There is no clock ticking away until you find someone new. This book asks the more important questions: Who will you be when you do find someone new? What new abilities (and tools) will you possess? How will you feel about yourself? What will you bring to the table? Hopefully not the unhealthy behaviors and patterns you brought last time. But let's not just hope. Because hope doesn't build healthy relationships. Let's make sure. Cement that shit by putting action behind your wants. Not just crossing your fingers and wishing things will be different this time.

So don't waste a single moment of your singlehood. This time is precious and valuable. Who knows when you'll be here again? It may be years, or decades. This book will make sure you squeeze every last drop out of this time by having you check in, process, challenge yourself, flip things on their head, and hold yourself accountable for thirty-one consecutive days.

Welcome to what may be the most significant part of your singlehood ride.

Because this is where you lay the tracks.

AUTHOR NOTE

I hate workbooks.
I hate journals.

They're like self-help video courses bought but never watched. Like gym memberships that never get used. The clutter of all those half-punched cards in a kitchen drawer. The first two pages are filled in, then the rest stay completely blank. The book binding never breaks. Workbooks sit under beds and sideways on top of bookshelves. Journals are left on nightstands collecting dust, some still wrapped in plastic. They have the life span of a New Year's resolution. Except these "resolutions" waste trees.

So when my publisher asked if I wanted to create a *Single on Purpose* workbook, my first thought was, *Hell no!* Then I sat with it a bit. What if I created a different type of workbook? What if it wasn't just a pretty journal with prompts and generic exercises pulled from a clinical cabinet? What if we don't even call it a workbook? What if it was an actual program, like what a coach gives an athlete training to compete? What if it was a daily tool to depend on, not something to just flip through and toss aside?

My answer to all these questions? If I were single, I would want a program. A legit tool. Something that parallels the concepts in the book but also gives me some fresh new lessons and insights.

That makes me want to open it daily. That brings me results if I follow the program. I would want it to be a daily implementation and ultimately a conduit into a real live community.

So this workbook is also an invitation. Because I wouldn't want to do this alone.

That's what I would want.

So that's what I created.

DISCLAIMER

This workbook is meant to drive you. Hard.

There should be dog-eared pages and nacho stains on every other page. Used like you felt in your last toxic relationship. Like all my books, this workbook will be honest and blunt and at times a little inappropriate. Like me. But it will make you feel something as well as give you structure. It's not just a workbook, it is a program. Handrails for your days. It will lay tracks for your singlehood journey. Some days it'll give you a push. Other days it'll hand you a mirror. I will be your therapist and singlehood coach for the next thirty-one days.

Like everything I write, I will come *with* you. Not *at* you. Sharing my own personal stories, challenges, and reflections.

DAY ONE

CONNECTION-TO-SELF ASSESSMENT

0 = never
1 = rarely
2 = sometimes
3 = frequently
4 = most often
5 = always

I can take myself out to dinner on a Friday night. And genuinely enjoy myself and not give a fuck.

0   1   2   3   4   5

I am able to communicate my needs and wants.

0   1   2   3   4   5

I am able to communicate my needs and wants in the bedroom.

0   1   2   3   4   5

I don't beat myself up if I'm not productive, if I don't work out, or if I eat something shitty.

0   1   2   3   4   5

I don't tie my worth to being in a relationship.

0   1   2   3   4   5

I forgive myself.

0   1   2   3   4   5

I talk to myself in a way that's respectful, compassionate, and kind. (I don't assassinate my character.)

0   1   2   3   4   5

I believe I bring a lot to the table in relationships.

0   1   2   3   4   5

I think I'm attractive. As a whole person. I know I'm not perfect, but I like myself and my body, and anyone would be lucky to have me.

0   1   2   3   4   5

I believe I'm lovable.

0   1   2   3   4   5

SCORING

0–10
It's time. To build a new foundation and a new relationship with yourself. The good news? The growth soil is the richest when you're single. It's time.

10–20
You may seek worth and validation from others more than you know, and that may be why your relationships have been lopsided. You struggle with your sense of self. We will work on that. Glad you're here.

20–30
Solid. Yes, there are things you can work on to connect more to yourself, but your foundation is strong. You've laid the groundwork. You're climbing the mountain. You just need to tip. And you will.

30–40
You have a good sense of self and worth. That means your connection to self is strong. Congratulations. Keep up the good work.

40–50
People like you are rare and have a smaller pool of potential partners to choose from because you know your worth and what you

believe you deserve. Your frustration may be less about yourself and more to do with the landscape of dating and swipe culture. Be patient. Be picky. And keep working on yourself. Your connection to self is not a light switch. It ebbs and flows and is ongoing. Like any relationship.

That was a quick assessment designed to spark a dialogue about your relationship with yourself. It is not truth. Your relationship with yourself is much more complicated than answering ten questions. This assessment is merely intended to check your temperature. So please do not label or judge or hold on to your "score" as truth. It was designed to make you think, to spark revelations. That is all.

DAY TWO

Every day from here on out will start with a mantra. Mantras are more than affirmations.

The word "mantra" is derived from two Sanskrit roots; *manas*, meaning "mind," and *tra*, meaning "tool." A mantra is a mind tool, but only if you create a bridge from your left brain (logic) to your right brain (feeling and being). Just repeating the words will keep you on the logic side.

So read the daily mantra and drop into your body. Feel the words like they're warm tea sipped on an empty stomach. Allow the message to seep into your body and veins. And remember, you're not holding on to the mantra. You are actually letting the words go. Repeating the words with white knuckles is holding on. Feeling the words flow through your body as you breathe is digesting. Letting go.

TODAY'S MANTRA

Love and relationships are only one part of my life. Not my entire life.

TODAY'S ONE THING

What's one thing you will *do* today to prove that your life is not just about love and relationships? It doesn't have to be some big terrifying action. It can be one small action. The first domino.

_____

_____

_____

_____

_____

_____

_____

_____

_____

_____

_____

_____

_____

_____

_____

_____

_____

_____

EXAMPLES

- [ ] Start sketching out what creating your own business would look like.

- [ ] Start a blog, a newsletter, or a book. Just write something honest.

- [ ] If you were to start a nonprofit, what would that look like? Start sketching it.

- [ ] Build something with your hands.

- [ ] Take on a new hobby or interest that you didn't have time for when you were in a relationship.

- [ ] Start a book club.

- [ ] Paint something, especially if you don't know how. Start a garden. Plant something.

- [ ] Plan a staycation.

- [ ] Take an online class on something you've always wanted to learn.

- [ ] Take a breath-work class (on- or offline).

- [ ] Try to make a new friend today.

- [ ] Research a topic you've always wanted to learn about. Take a deep dive.

- [ ] Read or listen to a new book. The entire thing. In one day.

- [ ] Prepare a meal slowly. Share it with someone. Learn how to bake.

- [ ] Explore your city. Go to a part of the city you rarely or never go to.

- [ ] Rescue a dog.

❏ Volunteer or sign up to volunteer soon.

❏ Start a podcast.

❏ Delete your dating apps.

❏ Redesign your apartment or living space. You don't have to do a complete remodel. Move furniture. Buy some flowers and candles or new art. Switch things up that feel good to you.

❏ Do something for someone else (anything).

Check anything you did from the list above or write about some other action you took.

_____

_____

_____

_____

_____

_____

_____

_____

_____

_____

_____

_____

_____

_____

TODAY'S SWEAT

What is your daily sweat today? It doesn't have to be a vigorous workout. It can be a hike, a yoga session, a walk—anything that gets you out of your head and into your body.

_____

_____

_____

_____

_____

_____

_____

WHY SWEAT?

It's not just about abs. Exercise feeds the brain. It increases blood flow, which is essential to delivering all the nutrients required to carry out the brain's job. It also increases the number of production molecules, which are important to brain function, including memory.

- Oxygen saturation and angiogenesis (blood vessel growth) occur in areas of the brain associated with rational thinking as well as with social, physical, and intellectual performance.

- Exercise reduces stress hormones and increases the number of neurotransmitters, like serotonin and norepinephrine, which are known to accelerate information processing.

- Exercise upregulates neurotrophins (brain-derived neurotrophic factor, insulin-like growth factor, and basic fibroblast growth factor). These support the survival and differentiation of neurons in the developing brain, dendritic branching, and synaptic machinery in the adult brain.

DAY THREE

I am not lonely. I am experiencing loneliness.

There is a difference between being lonely and experiencing loneliness. Being lonely is tied to your worth. Experiencing loneliness just means you are human.

TODAY'S
MANTRA

TODAY'S ONE THING

Describe the loneliness you are feeling. Think of it like having a cold or the flu. What does it feel like? What are the symptoms? What does loneliness feel like in your body? The more detailed you can be the better. As if you're explaining your experience to an alien who has no idea what loneliness is.

_____

_____

_____

_____

_____

_____

WHY DESCRIBE LONELINESS?

Yes, you probably haven't written your feels down since you carried that composition book in high school. Yes, I know you're still tempted to skip this part. But here's why it's important. Writing down what you're feeling or experiencing does three things: (1) It validates what you're feeling. What you're feeling is real. And there is acceptance in this validation. (2) Writing it down is processing it. Not just dumping out and unloading, but also working through, reflecting, and understanding yourself better. You are learning how you work. (3) You told yourself when you started this workbook you wouldn't half-ass it. If you're going to do it, go all the way. Any resistance is color dye showing you where you need to double down.

TODAY'S SWEAT

Take one class. Any class. Boxing. CrossFit. Yoga. It doesn't matter. If you already take daily fitness classes, take a different class. Most likely your gym has many different classes and you usually take the same one. Try something new. Flip the script. Switch it up. It's good for you.

DAY FOUR

Today I will practice self-care. Not in a cheesy cliché kind of way, but in a real honest-to-me practical but more importantly sustainable way.

TODAY'S
MANTRA

The term "self-care" has been turned into a trendy T-shirt that everyone's wearing just to fit in. Because working on yourself is cool now. But very few are actually practicing self-care. Posting filtered photos of green juice in a bubble bath or a facedown massage in Hawaii with a #lovemylife #finallylovemyself hashtag isn't self-care. That's called "I want you to think my life is great" and "I really do love myself." Real self-care doesn't require an announcement. It's something you do when no one's looking, like your morning shit. Like deciding to send your ex to voicemail. True self-care happens in moments. In the mundane. Self-care isn't a planned event that requires an airbnb and a good camera. Self-care doesn't require hashtags.

Redefine what self-care means to you. In *Single. On Purpose.* I talk about how I found myself through a motorcycle, barbells, and doughnuts. A hard sweaty workout pushing myself harder than I thought I could. Hitting flow states on two wheels and practicing pure presence. And allowing myself a treat once in a while because I deserved it. That was how I took care of and connected to myself. I never got on a plane and went on an exotic vacation. I didn't have the means. But even if I had, I don't know if travel would have been self-care for me at that time. I think that would have been me running away. Running away from self instead of toward self.

Practicing self-care means asking yourself what it is you need. Right now. Today. In this moment. But more importantly, it means asking yourself: *Do I have the ability to give that to myself?* Most people do not.

TODAY'S ONE THING

Write down your new definition of self-care. Really take a beat and think about this, because if you don't, society will define it for you. Things you have heard and seen about self-care may not be your truth. So focus on what *you* define as taking care of yourself. Remember, self-care is about taking care of yourself in order to build a better relationship with yourself.

_____

_____

_____

_____

_____

WHY DEFINE "SELF-CARE"?

Our definitions are what we pull from, whether consciously or unconsciously. They are ingrained and baked in. And if we don't redefine things once in a while, we are most likely pulling from a dishonest place. Every time we do that we are disconnecting with ourselves. Connection comes from pulling from our truth. New definitions give us that. It's how we break patterns and re-align ourselves.

I will ask you to redefine many things during these thirty-one days.

ONE *MORE* THING

Make a list of some self-care practices you will actually execute. Not things that sound good or clever. Real things you will do. Then write down how this practice will connect you to yourself. How is doing it self-care?

For example, here are a few of my self-care practices for this week:

- **Eating a sriracha roast beef sandwich at 8:30 in the morning while I work at a coffee shop** (happening right now as I write this). Although it breaks my intermittent fast, a sriracha roast beef sandwich is better than a chocolate croissant, which would have been my first choice. It's been a productive week, and I deserve this. Allowing myself to have this treat and being okay with it, not bashing myself on the way home, will connect me to myself because I usually don't allow it (which disconnects me from myself).

- **Taking an honest beat before answering a call/text/FaceTime.** I usually answer instinctively anytime someone rings me. I answer without thinking, though I often regret it. I get sucked into long conversations I don't want to have. Taking a beat and checking in with myself before answering to see whether I really want to or I'd rather send it to voicemail is practicing self-care.

- **Watering my lawn.** WTF? How is watering your lawn self-care? I haven't watered a lawn since the eighties, when my parents couldn't afford sprinklers. But recently, after purchasing my first home, in Altadena, I have put tons of effort into the backyard, and part of that is maintaining a thick, lush green lawn.

Although we have a sprinkler system, I started doing it myself at sunset. I noticed it calms me. So now I pop in earbuds and listen to nineties music. Watering the lawn has become therapeutic, and something I enjoy doing alone. Watering my lawn has become self-care.

Okay, your turn.

New self-care practices I will execute:

_____

_____

_____

_____

_____

_____

_____

_____

_____

_____

_____

_____

_____

_____

_____

_____

DAY FIVE

I will detach from my distorted thinking so I don't fall into a slippery well. Today I will detach to connect.

TODAY'S MANTRA

Our daily distorted thinking disconnects us from ourselves. From the time we wake up to the time we hit the pillow, our minds are spinning. I'm not talking about obsessing over your daily tasks and all the things you need to get done. I'm talking about your distorted thinking. All or nothing. Polarizing. Jumping to conclusions. Catastrophizing. Future tripping. Not living in the here and now. Living instead in what-ifs that emotionally weigh you down and turn your fish-tank (mind) dirty, forcing you to swim in your own shit.

When you're single, it's easier to fall into cognitive distortions. *What if I'm alone forever? What if I never find love again? What if I get too old to have babies? What if . . . what if . . . what if . . .*

TODAY'S ONE THING

Although there are three steps, it's just one thing.

STEP 1. Shine a bright light on your thoughts today.

STEP 2. Question your thoughts.

STEP 3. Notice recurring patterns in your thoughts.

EXTRA

Schedule your worry. Yes, you read that right. Sometimes the thoughts just need to be acknowledged, but once they are they lose their power. Set a timer for ten minutes and write down all of the distorted thoughts flying around in your head. All. Of. Them. When the alarm goes off, it's time to go back to your life.

Start your timer. Unload all your thoughts below. Without judgment.

_____

_____

_____

_____

_____

_____

TODAY'S SWEAT

Take a walk. That's it. Simple. It doesn't matter if you walk around the block or hike to a new city.

But you're not just walking. You're taking a mindfulness walk. No headphones. Instead, focus on what you see, hear, smell, and feel. Ground and anchor yourself using all your senses. Allow your thoughts to come and go and focus on just being present. Notice the natural world around you. Flowers, trees, birds. Feel the wind on your face and the energy of the spaces. If you see someone, make eye contact. Smile. Practice being human—being present.

DAY SIX

FUCK IT FRIDAY

It may not be Friday. But fuck it, that's okay.

When I was punching clocks instead of the sky, in every shitty job where I was overworked and underpaid I brought the team a giant box of doughnuts on Fridays. I said, "We work hard all week. Fuck it. It's Friday. Go at it!" It wasn't about the doughnuts. It was about allowing ourselves some grace, remembering we mattered. Yes, the grace came in the form of sugar, which was all I could afford in those days. But it wasn't about the doughnuts. It was about the meaning behind them. Since then, every Friday I give myself a treat. It doesn't have to be a doughnut. It can be stopping work early. Going to the beach. Taking a motorcycle ride. Rubbing one out. Whatever I feel I deserve that I don't give myself daily.

TODAY'S ONE THING

Pick one thing that you don't normally give yourself but you will today. Because you've worked hard and deserve it. Not because you're numbing or eating your feelings.

EXAMPLES

- Leave or stop work early.
- Take yourself out to your favorite restaurant.
- Get a mani/pedi.
- Go to a museum.
- Eat a doughnut.
- Go for a motorcycle ride.
- Sit at a coffee shop and read or write.
- Make art.
- Go to the beach.
- Take a long bath.
- Get a massage.
- Do takeout and Netflix.
- Take yourself to a concert.
- Sign up for a dance class.
- Take a staycation.
- Go to a Korean spa.

DAY SEVEN

The call is coming from inside the house. The call is coming from inside the house. The call is coming from inside the house.

TODAY'S MANTRA

And until you answer it, the disconnect between you and who you are is going to haunt you. No perfect partner can answer that call for you.

TODAY'S ONE THING

All the negative beliefs you have about yourself are not just in-securities. We all have insecurities. I think my nose is too wide. I wish I was taller. Those are insecurities. Negative beliefs go deeper. These are core beliefs about yourself that stem from your childhood, upbringing, family, traumatic life experiences, and previous relationships.

Here are a few of mine:

- I'm an *almost* guy. I can take something to the ninety-nine-yard line but can't make the touchdown.

- I'm a hack writer. I got lucky.

- I'm too old to be a dad.

TIPS

Try to uncover your underlying beliefs. Think about the labels you've put on yourself because of your story. Think about your job. What is the label you always give yourself? Look at your childhood family dynamic. How did you not fit in? What labels did you create for yourself because of that experience growing up? What about the labels for yourself you have with friends?

_____

_____

_____

_____

_____

_____

DAILY SWEAT

Pick one exercise you hate doing or are not good at. For many it's burpees. For me it's running. Incorporate this exercise into your daily sweat. Don't just go through the motions of doing it with a poor attitude. Make a true effort and see if you can get better at it.

_____

_____

_____

_____

_____

_____

DAY EIGHT

Today I will prove myself wrong.

TODAY'S
MANTRA

TODAY'S ONE THING

Take your list of false and limited beliefs about yourself and now write down where those beliefs came from. It's time to see how the movie was made. The more you understand the more you'll see that your beliefs were fabricated. Prove yourself wrong.

Then write down what is actually true and what your distorted thought pattern is.

For example, here's mine.

- **I'M AN ALMOST GUY. I CAN TAKE SOMETHING TO THE NINETY-NINE-YARD LINE BUT CAN'T SCORE THE TOUCH-DOWN.** This belief comes from so many of my projects and opportunities coming close but not succeeding. Years and years of this made me believe I am an *almost* person, a half-ass. I believe I can start projects but can't finish them or make them successful.

- What I'm not considering or giving value to are all the things that actually did happen but that I don't classify as big or life changing. Smaller things I built or accomplished that eventually led to big and life changing. My unhealthy thought pattern is minimizing my accomplishments and putting weight only on big shiny things. In looking back, I see that big things not working out was actually guidance. They needed to not work out if I was going to pivot, learn, grow, reposition myself to keep swimming toward my true north. I would not be who I am today had those big shiny things happened. I would be the douchebag in the Ferrari.

- **I'M A FAILED WRITER.** I spent a decade pursuing screenwriting and not being able to turn it into a career. I became a therapist because I failed as a writer. Did I actually fail as a screenwriter, or did the universe have different plans for my writing? Was screenwriting just a runway for my flight? My distorted thought pattern valued only one type of writing and minimized my career as an author.

- **I'M TOO OLD TO BE A GOOD DAD.** This negative belief buys into societal time lines. Defining a good dad as a young man in his twenties and thirties instead of a man with capacity and emotional intelligence. The truth is, I would have been an absent father in my twenties and thirties. I was a child myself, lacking emotional tools. I was reactive and unhappy. I am a better father today because I am older. My distorted thought pattern is tying what it looks like to be a good father to youth and energy over capacity and life wisdom.

Your turn.

_____

_____

_____

_____

_____

_____

_____

_____

_____

DAY NINE

It's Marie Kondo Day. Or in my words: *Put your life through a strainer.*

I will get rid of anything in my life that doesn't produce joy.

Quick story.

I recently purchased some generic underwear, the kind that comes in a five-pack. It's just underwear. Who cares, right? Well, these boxer briefs are a tad too tight and cut like nineties Britney Spears low-rise jeans, so you can see the top of my ass crack. And since they're also low in the front, I now have a small muffin top. They're not bad enough to not wear, but they

TODAY'S
MANTRA

also don't make me feel comfortable and sexy. They're just there and make sense. They're cheap and practical, one solid dark color.

But here's the thing. I'm wearing them all day. Over time they'll start to bother me like a tiny pebble in my shoe that I can't seem to get out. I'll have to keep pulling them up and feel self-conscious about people seeing my ass crack when I do squats at the gym.

So I decided to toss them. All of them. And I bought new fancy ones that fit my body perfectly and come in different colors and patterns. One pair cost as much as the generic five-pack. But they make me feel calm and comfortable, and my butt looks good in them. No more pebble in my shoe.

Joy isn't just about producing a shot of happy. It's also about contributing to your daily comfort. So you're not living in subtle discomfort or panic. Joy is about changing your state. By removing the pebble from your shoe, or the thorns from your side. Joy elevates your mood. It's an energy thing. Even if it's just a little boost, applying this mindset and making it non-negotiable across your entire life, not just with your underwear, will connect you more to yourself.

Finding joy is a form of self-care. So no more tolerating. No more doing things because they make sense or are practical. Life doesn't live in practical. That's where fear lives.

TODAY'S ONE THING

Go through your closet. Toss or donate anything that doesn't make you feel good about yourself. If it's neutral, get rid of it. Only keep what you love. Or as Marie Kondo would say, what sparks joy.

Watch an episode of *Tidying Up* with Marie Kondo if you want to visually see what this looks like. You will also realize it's not easy. You will want to hold on to things because you paid a lot for them, or because you see no logical reason to get rid of them. You will want to hold on to things because they're attached to memories. You will fight with yourself. But if something doesn't spark joy, toss it. Remember, you are shedding and this is a part of the process.

CHECKLIST

❏ Underwear   ❏ Sweats

❏ Shirts   ❏ Workout clothes

❏ Socks   ❏ Hats

❏ Dresses   ❏ Glasses

❏ Shoes   ❏ Sunglasses

❏ Jackets   ❏ Jewelry

Go through it all.

DAILY SWEAT

Go on a hike. Get out in nature. Notice trees. Use your senses to anchor yourself. Try to stay out of your head. Listen to music or a podcast if that helps. You don't have to wear a weight vest, but it shouldn't be a stroll. Make sure you get sweaty.

DAY TEN

I will not settle anymore.

As I mentioned yesterday, you are putting your life through a strainer and your wardrobe is only a small part of your life. That was the warm-up. Now the heavy lifting. Or maybe yesterday was heavy lifting, depending on your relationship with your clothes and things. Today may be easier. Either way, both days are imperative to rebuilding a rich life space so your relationship with yourself improves.

TODAY'S MANTRA

TODAY'S ONE THING

MEANING: Write in the meaning circle below everything in your life that has meaning. For each item, ask yourself:

Is it meaningful to you?

Does it line up with your story?

JOY: Write in the joy circle below everything in your life that brings you joy. For each item, ask yourself:

Does it light you up?

Does it produce joy?

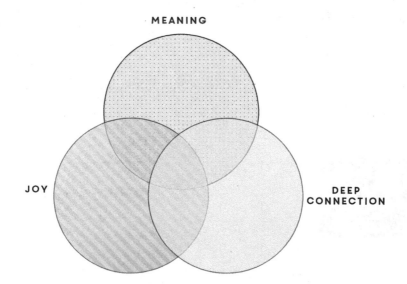

If it's a person, are you passionate about this relationship? Or do you just hang on to it because of your history? For example, your sister may have meaning in your life because she is family, but that relationship may not bring you joy. You may actually not even like her. If there's no deep connection between you, she would go only in the meaning circle.

DEEP CONNECTION. Write in the deep connection circle above all the ways in which you currently find deep connection, both to yourself and to others. For each item, ask yourself:

Does this person or thing produce a deep connection to yourself or to others?

Does this thing or person make you feel drained? Or energized and fulfilled?

TODAY'S JOURNALING

_____

_____

_____

_____

_____

What changes do you need to make to have more meaning, joy, and deep connection in your life?

_____

_____

_____

_____

_____

Do you feel like you are settling in your life? In what areas?

_____

_____

_____

_____

_____

What would it look like to not settle anymore? What would need to change for that to happen?

_____

_____

_____

_____

_____

_____

I will hang my life on meaning, joy, and deep connections.

Okay, so yesterday sucked. If you're anything like me when I was single, you either wrote a bunch of bullsh*t in those circles and moved on or you were faced with the grim reality that your life is severely lacking in all three departments. That's okay. Single-hood is about building. Not judging. And the first step to building is writing down what you want.

TODAY'S
MANTRA

TODAY'S ONE THING

First, let's start wide.

What do you want more of in your life? Go wild. There is no right or wrong answer. Just splatter paint. Write whatever comes to mind. When you write without thinking, you are tapping into something deeper and you'll find out things about yourself that you didn't know. Surprise yourself.

_____

_____

_____

_____

_____

_____

Here's my list.

- Patience
- REM sleep
- Tattoos
- Meditation
- Motorcycle rides
- Man dates
- Like-minded people
- Vegetables

- Adventure
- Magical moments
- Good books
- Good coffee
- Good dark chocolate
- Breath
- Bubble baths
- Gratitude

- Serendipity
- Uncontrollable laughter
- Acceptance
- Courage
- Faith
- Sharper intuition
- Trust in the universe
- Grounding
- Travel
- Date nights
- Self-compassion
- Mindfulness

- Revelations
- Unexpected breezes
- Expensive candles
- Deep intimacy
- High-thread-count sheets
- Pants that fit
- Certainty
- New definitions
- New perspectives
- New experiences
- Therapy

What do you want less of?

_____

_____

_____

_____

_____

_____

_____

_____

_____

Here's my list.

- Negativity
- Shoulds
- Gossip
- Empty promises
- Loud Uber drivers
- Thoughts that keep me in yesterday
- Lopsided friendships
- Loose socks
- Road rage
- Limiting beliefs
- Fast food
- Speeding tickets
- Cheap underwear
- Music that doesn't make me feel anything
- Checklists
- Guilt for things I shouldn't feel guilty about
- Excuses
- Voicemail messages

- Supermarket sushi
- Inflated egos
- Plastic plants
- Judgment
- Toxic spaces
- Time lines
- Carpet
- Posturing
- Self-doubt
- Approval/validation
- OPP (other people's problems)
- Anxiety about student loans
- Fortune cookies with generic fortunes
- The middle seat in planes
- Opinions on how I should live my life
- Anything that doesn't line up with my truth or purpose
- Fear

Now let's tighten the vice. This time think about it. Analyze. Consider.

List the kinds of meaningfulness you want in your life.

_____

_____

_____

_____

_____

List the joys you want in your life.

_____

_____

_____

_____

_____

List the deep connections you want in your life.

_____

_____

_____

_____

_____

TODAY'S LISTEN

You know when I'm single because I usually have earbuds in my ears. In coffee shops, in restaurants, when I'm doing dishes and chores, when I'm walking around town. I am constantly feeding my brain and I find audio to be the best way to do it.

Maybe it's research and science or self-care or just something fucking funny. Because you haven't laughed out loud in a while. Choose any topic you want. The brain is like a muscle. We must exercise it often. Learn something new today. Or something that makes you feel something.

Suggestion: *Single on Purpose* podcast. I have rotating hosts and wellness experts three times a week (myself included). But more important, your stories at the end. Real true life singlehood stories of people going through what you're going through. Find it wherever you listen to podcasts.

DAY TWELVE

I will get off my island. Or I'll always be Tom Hanks talking to a volleyball.

TODAY'S MANTRA

TODAY'S ONE THING

Make a new friend today. Okay, let's be realistic. You're probably not going to ask someone to sit down and have coffee and crepes with you for an hour. Or you may. I don't know. But making a new friend starts with an intention and one action step. That action step can be a simple "hello." A smile. Any form of engagement that's appropriate but also requires you to step out of your comfort zone.

When we're in a relationship, yes, we may have friends, but we don't make an effort to make new ones. We don't feel it's necessary, but then we realize our current friendships only hang on history and we don't really have much in common anymore. The truth is, we should always be making new friends. Forever. Because friendships change as we change. Like our intimate relationships, they can expire. So if we don't make an effort to always make new friends, we will feel alone. New friendships are a must, *especially* when we're in a relationship.

TIP: Kill two birds with one stone. When you're taking a fitness class, yoga class, or salsa dancing lessons, or doing anything community based, make an effort to befriend someone. Your effort doesn't have to be forced. It can be organic, but you do have to make it. Say "hi," start a conversation. Engage. Challenge yourself, especially if you're an introvert like me.

How did you try to make a new friend today?

_____

_____

_____

_____

_____

_____

How did you feel about it?

_____

_____

_____

_____

_____

DAILY SWEAT

Take an in-person class. Any class, but not your usual class. A class with new people you don't know. Sweat with strangers, and before, during, or after, engage with someone socially. At your own pace.

DAY THIRTEEN

I am not moving on. I am moving *through.*

TODAY'S ONE THING

Write a forgiveness letter to yourself. I know that can sound cheesy, but it's actually really powerful. Think about all the relationships you've been in, the good, the bad, and the ugly. But instead of thinking about the other person, think about how *you* showed up. Your intention, energy, behavior, words. What do you want to forgive yourself for?

WHY FORGIVE YOURSELF?

One of the things we hold on to the tightest, creating emotional residue, is what we have done in past relationships, how we treated someone, or how we allowed someone to treat us. Forgiveness is not a light switch. It is a daily practice. Some days it's easy to forgive and some days it's hard. But many of us have not even started the process. We may have thought about forgiving ourselves. But we have not incorporated it into our daily lives. This exercise will force you to examine how you showed up and help you deploy compassion. It will help you understand where you were mentally and emotionally at that time in your life and why you did what you did. Forgiveness is the beginning of letting go.

Be transparent.

Be honest.

Be thorough.

Here's my letter.

I forgive myself for not having the discipline or control in my twenties to hold off on sex before marriage, as she wanted. My hormones were bouncing off the walls. I didn't have a strong sense of self. I was searching. I was codependent. I was young. I was impatient and impulsive. My heart was in the right place even if I didn't have the tools to hold a safe space. I forgive myself for hanging the relationship over Georgia's head and putting pressure on her to love me in a way she wasn't ready for.

I forgive myself for being insensitive with Georgia. For loving her with judgment. For not truly seeing her. For trying to mold her into someone she wasn't. I forgive myself for being hypocritical and not showing up in the way I write about. I was still unhappy in my own life. As she called out. I forgive myself for ending it abruptly. For once again being reactive. For not treating her heart as precious.

I forgive myself for ending the relationship with Street Art without doing any real work. For not doing anything when I heard she wasn't in a good place and spiraling downward. I forgive myself for starting something with someone else too soon and blaming it on the moon. I forgive myself for taking the easy way out. For leaving her with a rent she couldn't afford. For not processing my drift.

Your turn.

_____

_____

_____

_____

_____

_____

_____

_____

_____

_____

_____

_____

_____

_____

_____

_____

_____

_____

_____

_____

Inhale the past, exhale forgiveness.

Take a deep inhale through your nose and count for three slow seconds, filling your belly and then your chest with air. Hold your breath for three slow seconds.

Now slowly exhale, releasing all the air. Imagine that the air in your body is colored red and you're trying to get all the red out. Repeat this breathing sequence. Inhale deeply for the count of three. Hold for three seconds. Exhale all the air until you have no more air. Then release even more.

Now as you inhale, think about all the things you carry from your previous relationships. The anger, the hurt, the regret. The blame, the internalization, the false beliefs about yourself and worth.

And let. Them. All. Go.

Repeat.
Repeat.
Repeat.

DAY FOURTEEN

I will take ownership, knowing that ownership is the soil for growth. Without it, self-forgiveness is illusive.

TODAY'S MANTRA

TODAY'S ONE THING

Ownership. What does taking ownership look like for you? In action. Not just words. Because forgiving yourself can also be a cop-out. Yes, forgive yourself for the things you still beat yourself up about. But also take ownership. What does taking ownership look like for you?

_____

_____

_____

_____

_____

_____

_____

_____

_____

_____

_____

_____

_____

_____

_____

_____

TODAY'S MEDITATION

Compassion meditation. It's different from other forms. Mindfulness meditation focuses on breathing to develop an awareness of the present moment. By contrast, compassion meditation focuses your attention in specific ways rather than letting your mind wander. Compassion meditation can, for example, be silently repeating benevolent phrases, or visualizing kind wishes that express the intention to move from judgment or dislike to caring, compassion, and understanding of another person.

WHY COMPASSION MEDITATION?

Compassion meditation improves mood, encourages more altruistic behavior, reduces anger and stress, and decreases maladaptive mind wandering, according to recent research. A 2013 study at the VA Puget Sound Health Care System in Seattle found that practicing loving-kindness meditation (a form of compassion meditation) for twelve weeks reduced symptoms of posttraumatic stress disorder as well as anger and depression among veterans with PTSD.

A 2005 study from Duke University Medical Center found that practicing loving-kindness meditation for eight weeks reduced pain and psychological distress among patients with chronic low back pain.

A 2015 study from Brazil found that practicing yoga along with compassion meditation three times a week for eight weeks improved quality of life, vitality, attention, and self-compassion among family caregivers of patients with Alzheimer's disease.

In a 2008 study, researchers from the University of Wisconsin–Madison, using functional magnetic resonance imaging (fMRI) scans, found that the brain circuitry that detects emotions and feelings, including empathy, is altered in people who have extensive experience practicing compassion meditation.

Set a timer for ten minutes. Sit or lie down, whichever is more comfortable for you. Pick the exes you have unresolved issues with. That you have anger and resentment toward. Play their story, their childhood, how they grew up, their high school and college years, their twenties. Most likely you know their story. Play it until they are the age they were when you had a relationship with them.

Can you humanize your exes knowing where they came from and what they experienced? Can you see why they were the way they were? Can you practice compassion? Can you wish them a good life? Can you love and accept them from a distance? Can you be angry *and* still wish them well? Can you practice compassion? Open your hands. No more white knuckles. Open your heart. Throw love at your exes. Instead of hate.

DAY FIFTEEN

I will return what I've been carrying around, like a pair of bowling shoes, from previous relationships. It does not belong to me.

TODAY'S MANTRA

TODAY'S ONE THING

Put an *X* in the box for the truths that you relate to. Also create your own.

- ❏ I was young and didn't have the tools to build something healthy.
- ❏ I will not allow previous love experiences to prevent me from creating new ones.
- ❏ The trust stove is not hot. I just think it is because I've been burned. The stove is off. I can trust again.
- ❏ I will not generalize about all men (all women) because I have been hurt by a few individuals.
- ❏ I am a different person today, with more wisdom and greater capacity.
- ❏ I bring more to the table than I ever have.
- ❏ Being single just means I have choices now.
- ❏ Not being in a relationship doesn't mean I am worth less.
- ❏ I will love myself first, always.
- ❏ I deserve healthy love.
- ❏ I deserve more. I deserve better. And I will create that for myself.
- ❏ My character arc is of great value. The things I've gone through have made me who I am.
- ❏ I can write a new story.
- ❏ I am grateful for all my love experiences, good or bad. They have taught me invaluable lessons and contributed to my evolution.

- ❏ I will not allow dating apps to make me feel like shit.

- ❏ I still believe in the magic of love.

- ❏ Love is all-encompassing. It is a way of being. Not something to search for.

- ❏ I will smash my internal ticking clock. I will take the pressure off myself to find love.

- ❏ I will attract. Not chase.

- ❏ I have more to give today because of what I have gone through.

- ❏ Barbie never needed Ken. All she needed was that fucking Vette.

- ❏ I have non-negotiables and I will hold them with two hands. No matter how hot the other person is, or how good the sex is, or how in love I am.

- ❏ I will work the shit out of this workbook because it's me investing in myself.

- ❏ I will create ten more self-encouraging coping thoughts of my own.

1 _____

2 _____

3 _____

4 _____

5 _____

6 _____

7 _____

8 _____

9 _____

10 _____

DAILY SWEAT

Row, cycle, swim, or run. This sweat is about endurance. As you're going, think about your story. All the shit you've gone through, how far you've come, how you've been treated in previous relationships. What you've put up with and are no longer willing to tolerate. Look at your character arc as if it were a movie. Leverage your story to motivate and push yourself when you get tired. See how far you can go.

DAY SIXTEEN

Love means compromise. But not compromise of self.

TODAY'S MANTRA

TODAY'S ONE THING

Time to do a relationship inventory. What did you tolerate in your previous relationships?

- ❏ Character assassination
- ❏ Lying
- ❏ Meaningless sex
- ❏ Losing my friends
- ❏ Gaslighting
- ❏ Being controlled
- ❏ Enmeshment
- ❏ Not being seen
- ❏ Not being heard

- ❏ Jealousy behavior
- ❏ Complacency
- ❏ Rejection
- ❏ Distance
- ❏ Unfulfilled promises
- ❏ Intimidation
- ❏ Self-rejection
- ❏ Loss of time

What else?

_____

_____

_____

_____

_____

How did tolerating these things affect your relationship with yourself? Explain for each.

_____

_____

_____

_____

_____

DAY SEVENTEEN

I will no longer negotiate things that are important to me and my growth. Because that shit didn't work the last time.

TODAY'S
MANTRA

TODAY'S ONE THING

Creating your non-negotiables.

Your non-negotiables give you the framework for your new life container. Love (healthy or not) has caused you, like many people, to negotiate things that were important to you and your growth. By negotiating these things, you slowly lost your sense of self. Maybe even your life. I started your list with a few I think everyone should hold on to.

What are your non-negotiables in each category of your life? I've listed a few of my own to get you started.

LOVE AND RELATIONSHIPS

- I will not be in an abusive relationship.
- I will not be with someone who does not have the ability to communicate in a healthy way.
- I will not fake orgasms anymore.

FRIENDSHIPS

- I will not be in lopsided friendships.
- I will no longer be the person who has to bring everyone together every time.
- I will make an effort to make new friends, even if I already have a lot of friends.

WORK AND CAREER

- I will not work in a job I'm not passionate about. If I'm currently in a passionless job, I will start building a bridge to the kind of job I want by doing everything I can to find something new that lights me up. Until I can leave this job and cross over to that one.

- I will not work for a boss who doesn't treat humans well.

- I will not be overworked and underpaid.

_____

_____

_____

_____

_____

_____

_____

_____

_____

_____

_____

_____

_____

_____

_____

_____

_____

DAILY SWEAT

Death by burpees. Remember, there is no rebirth without death. So I *highly* recommend doing burpees until you can't. Until you are drenched—not just with one bead of sweat trickling down your forehead but when your shirt is wet and your ass is dripping with sweat. That might be ten burpees, or it might be a hundred. (Check it out on YouTube if you don't know what a burpee is.)

Yes, I know you hate burpees. As you are doing them, remember the Hero's Journey. In the beginning you will go from comfort to discomfort. Then, at some point, you will want to stop. That's your dragon. Slay it. You may have to slay many dragons as your mind tries to convince you to quit. Things will come up. It may get emotional. You may get angry. That's okay. Lean into the anger, knowing that when you finish you will be coming back to the village changed. You'll be a slightly different person, with a new mindset. This is not just a workout. It's a template for life.

STAMP YOUR SWEAT

Stamp your sweat in the box below. Your hand, face, ass, doesn't matter. What matters is that you earned it. This stamp is proof that you're working hard on yourself.

DAY EIGHTEEN

A reset doesn't mean I'm weak or that I've stopped. It actually means the complete opposite. Today I will reset.

TODAY'S
MANTRA

TODAY'S ONE THING
Reset.

After my divorce, I told myself I was either buying a motorcycle—which I've always wanted but never gave myself permission to have, mostly because whoever I was with thought they were too dangerous—or taking a trip to Italy, since I've never really been out of LA (kind of embarrassing as a thirty-five-year-old at the time). I ended up doing both. What I learned in Italy was that Italians take breaks. A whole city will shut down around noon and everyone will take a nap. Businesses close for a couple hours. It was mind blowing. Italians take resets seriously.

So when I got back I started practicing resets. Threaded them into my daily life. The first thing I noticed was the guilt I felt. Like I was slacking off, being lazy and unproductive. Then I realized that feeling came from my programming. It was an important reminder of how much culture forms us.

Today I find a daily reset to be mandatory. I don't necessarily shut down work and force myself to nap every day. A reset can vary, depending on what I feel I need and can give myself that day.

Here are what some of my resets look like:

- A thirty-minute walk
- An afternoon nap

- A motorcycle ride
- A cappuccino on the patio at one of my favorite coffee spots
- A meditation
- A quick swim in my pool followed by an air-dry on the sunny deck
- A hard CrossFit workout (yes, believe it or not, that calms me)
- A meaningful conversation with a friend, by phone or in person
- A hot tub or ice bath spa session
- A pedicure, with the phone off

What does a reset look like for you?

_____

_____

_____

_____

_____

_____

_____

_____

_____

_____

_____

_____

DAILY SWEAT

Rest day. No workout or movement today. On purpose.

DAY NINETEEN

It's impossible to be curious and judgmental at the same time. Today I will practice curiosity.

TODAY'S ONE THING

Get curious.

Judgment stunts our potential. Shrinks our heart. Locks up our gifts. If we don't actively practice nonjudgment, we will default to judging. We've been conditioned that way. It's just the world we live in.

I used to be a very judgmental person in my twenties. I judged what people did for a living, what they wore, what they drove, who they chose to love, etc. Which means I also judged myself. This constant judgment made me feel miserable. Today, when I feel myself judging, whether myself or others, I take a beat and see if I can pull from curiosity instead.

In what areas or relationships do you find yourself being the most judgmental? What people do you judge the most? What situations?

What would it look like to be curious instead about who or what you're judging?

_____

_____

_____

_____

_____

_____

DAILY SWEAT

Do something you've been curious about but also judgmental and perhaps self-conscious about. Maybe you don't want people to know you do this activity. For me, it would be Pilates. Because I judge and label it. For many others, it would be CrossFit.

DAY TWENTY

I will not blame myself for how I have loved. Because love is not the same. It changes as we change.

TODAY'S
MANTRA

TODAY'S ONE THING
Stop the blaming.

Many people don't realize that not all love is the same. So they blame themselves for love that was never set up to be healthy. But they're not being fair to themselves.

For example, love at first sight usually isn't love. It's lust. It's a strong animalistic attraction formed from the energy we give off from our story plus our firm grip on love stories from movies and fairy tales. I understand that you can see someone across a room, lock eyes, and a few months later move in together, adopt a dog, and tie the knot. These things happen. It happened to me. But that's not love at first sight. The love doesn't come until later, and it's usually a rocky love. Or it isn't love at all. It's stretched attraction, a tornado of chaos. He's Sid and you're Nancy.

At second sight, you may find a person attractive without necessarily thinking you found your soulmate. Your socks are still on. But you're curious and willing to make an effort. It's a gradual build. You have more power this time. Logic is still accessible. You have not lost yourself. Or your life. You've held on to your ability to make healthier choices. And those healthier choices keep the relationship on track, keep it from veering off the road and nosediving into a ditch. Basically, there's a much better chance of this relationship having legs.

Third sight means you've invested in the connection and swum past the breakers. You've pulled the curtain back, seen the skeletons, and still want to invest. You've also explored your own activation and what comes up. But you also let things happen organically. Like a leaf unfolding from a bud, you see more and more growth not only in the relationship but also in yourself because of the relationship. It's greater than you. The two of you are Harry and Sally. Not Sid and Nancy. The potential of this turning into something sustainable increases exponentially. When attraction grows from 360- and 30,000-foot views and consistency, it has wings as well as legs.

I've experienced all three. I think age plays a factor as well. When we're in our teens and twenties, we're only looking for that first-sight love, or maybe second-sight love. We don't sit in the uncomfortable. We only search for exciting, fresh, and instant. It's not until later, after many hours of therapy and possibly a rebirth, that we realize real love takes work. We also finally understand that the kind of attraction that makes your legs wobble usually points to dysfunction. If it seems too good to be true, it usually is. Unless the "too good" is what the two of you have built.

TODAY'S JOURNALING

In what past relationships do you still blame yourself for how it turned out? What exactly do you blame yourself for?

_____

_____

_____

_____

_____

_____

How does this blame from a past relationship affect your relationship with yourself today?

_____

_____

_____

_____

_____

What are some ways you can stop blaming yourself?

_____

_____

_____

_____

_____

DAY TWENTY-ONE

Trusting that things will happen in their own time will be my practice.

TODAY'S
MANTRA

TODAY'S ONE THING

Smash the clock. In the clock below, write down everything you have tightly tied to society's ticking clock and made yourself, in doing so, feel anxious, panicked, and less than. For example, have you put marriage, having a baby, buying a house, or grad school on a time line?

DAILY SWEAT/LISTEN HYBRID

To get away from the time lines, avoid being trapped by "clocks" in the future, and stay in the here and now, drop into your body and lungs and the movement of your choice. It can be whatever movement you want to do today. But as you move, listen to these episodes of my podcast. They all relate to smashing your inner clock.

"It's Okay to Not Know"

"Stop Creating What Was"

"Live Like You're on Vacation"

DAY TWENTY-TWO

I will not exchange my truth for membership.

TODAY'S
MANTRA

TODAY'S ONE THING

This was one of the most important promises I made to myself after my divorce. I realized that I had spent most of my life exchanging my truth for membership in something external, like approval, validation, love, or money. And that made me live an outside-in life instead of an inside-out life. Exchanging my truth for membership lowered my potential and grayed me out. I felt false and powerless. I stayed caught in a chasing state instead of an attracting state.

What are you exchanging for membership these days?

At work

_____

_____

In dating

_____

_____

With friends

_____

_____

With family

_____

_____

In society

_____

_____

DAILY STRETCH

Stretching is one thing I know I need to do more of but always forget or put off doing. But it's imperative. You can't get stronger without being more flexible. So today we stretch. You can do it on your own or take a yoga class. Whatever you prefer. But just make sure it's a legit stretch, at least thirty minutes. Don't forget to breathe.

DAY TWENTY-THREE

I am not what I went through. My experiences don't define me. I am more than what happened.

TODAY'S
MANTRA

TODAY'S ONE THING

Dissolve your limited beliefs about yourself. Our false and limited beliefs about ourselves stem from our experiences, which we have internalized and tied to our worth. It's important to know what these beliefs are and where they come from.

For example:

I AM NOT GOOD ENOUGH. From my upbringing—my parents never telling me I was enough.

I AM NOT LOVABLE. From all the toxic relationships I've had in my life.

I WILL NEVER BE IN A HEALTHY RELATIONSHIP. From never being in a healthy relationship.

What are your false beliefs and where do they come from?

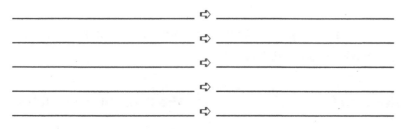

How does each false belief ripple into your life?

For example, the ripple effect of falsely believing I'm not lovable has been my tendency to sabotage relationships.

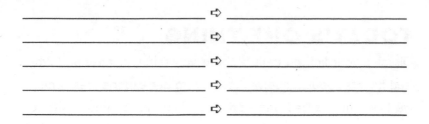

There is no right way to dissolve false beliefs. Do what works for you. Give yourself new experiences. Distinguish the different voices enforcing those beliefs and know where they are coming from. Do affirmations. Challenge your beliefs. Put on your detective hat and look for proof that your beliefs about yourself are true.

This a huge topic, with many doors in. But you have to dissolve false beliefs in ways that work for you. Ways that are sustainable and can be a daily practice. No matter what technique you use, what's important is that you use it. And the only sustainable way is to thread it into your daily life.

What's one thing you will thread into your life to start dissolving your false and limited beliefs?

The Belief   **The One Thing You'll Do**

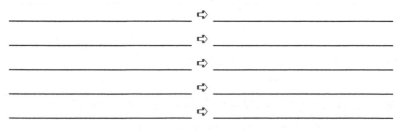

DAILY SWEAT

Today's sweat is less about movement and more about environ-
ment. Hike or walk in nature. Submerge yourself in trees, dirt,
rocks, trails with fresh air and views. Nature grounds us and
calms the nervous system. Take a nature bath today.

DAY TWENTY-FOUR

My worth is decided by me, not by others.

TODAY'S ONE THING

List everything that makes you unique and valuable. What do you bring to the table as a human being? Think about how you are and how you show up. Not just what you can do. These are things that you like about yourself. But they can also be lined with judgment. Some of the things I like about myself today were things I hated about myself in the past. So liking things about yourself requires a journey. It took me over a decade to like these things about myself:

- My inappropriateness sometimes
- Having way more ideas than I will ever have time to execute
- Being high-strung
- Always building the bus while I'm driving it

- Being early to everything
- Talking too much
- Writing fast
- Being a tad off-center
- Super-dry sense of humor
- Thirst for adventure
- Favorite color being gray

Your turn.

_____

_____

_____

_____

_____

_____

DAY TWENTY-FIVE

Today I will acknowledge how far I've come. Because I rarely do. All the shit I went through. All the redos and having to start all over. Dodging all the kitchen sinks life has thrown at me. Getting hit.

TODAY'S MANTRA

Going down. Standing
up. Getting hit. Going
down. Standing up.
And I'm still standing.
With more wisdom
and a shit-eating grin.
I will acknowledge
my courage, my
persistence, and my
belief in my story.

TODAY'S ONE THING

Imagine getting a letter from your future self. The person you'll be five years from now. After going through everything you're going through these days and the learnings that will come from that. Like who you are today because of everything you went through in the past. Take a minute and really drop into your body. Feel who that person will be. How will that person think and behave? What kind of energy will that person have? What limited beliefs will this person no longer carry? Then write a letter from that person. From you in the future to you now.
Here's mine.

Dear Chul Ki [my Korean name],
I want you to know that you will be in a good place. Everything you're currently worried about is wasted energy and residue from an unnurtured nervous system and trying to force life to happen on your terms. As you continue to work on your relationship with yourself, as you sit with yourself, breathe, and look inward as well as up (asking yourself how you can be of service), you will naturally take more "I's" out of your sentences. Things may not unfold exactly how you imagined, but they will unfold as they are meant to. You need to start trusting that. You will realize you need less and appreciate everything you have and how far you've come. This will change that nasty default you go to: panic and unworthiness. So stop forcing life to happen the way you want it to. Let things go. Let things grow. Also, stop cutting your hair and keep that merm (man perm). It works for you.

Here are a few important reminders to help you along the way.

Quit chasing. There is a difference between pursuing your goals and being in a constant state of chase. You've been chasing something most of your life, and it causes nothing but anxiety and feeling less than. You know this. Stop fighting or forcing the current. Instead, let it take you. Things will happen when they're supposed to happen. Do the best you can each day and be okay with it, knowing that as long as you are making decisions that are honest to you, your path will unfold.

Don't be concerned with what others think. There's a big difference between care and concern. You're going to care. You're human. Not everyone will like you. Some will even say it. It will hurt. You will heal. But if you hold on to it, you will be making other people's opinions of you a concern. By doing this, you will be allowing other people to write your story instead of writing it yourself. Don't be consumed with what other people think. Remember, it's only their version of your story.

Continue to dream big, often, and awake. The way you did most of sixth period. It's okay to do that now. The more the better. What you dream is where you will go. That is your compass. Don't be afraid to dream, no matter how big or ridiculous you may think your dreams are. You are painting your life. Don't do it by numbers. Splash. Color outside the lines.

If you're rich, remember that man makes the money, but money doesn't make the man. If you're poor, remember that man makes the money, but money doesn't make the man.

Know that you are a special blend. Everything that's happened to you is what makes you *YOU*, and no one can take that away.

That is a gift, not a curse. Know the value of it. Your story is what makes you rare, not defective. So quit trying to rip out chapters. Just focus on writing new ones.

Breathe. You've always had trouble with this. Keep reminding yourself to take longer and deeper breaths.

Be kind. Life is too short to be an asshole. Especially to the people close to you. You have resting bitch face so you have to be extra kind. If you don't like someone, always look inward first. Eliminate hate. It's wasted energy and will only poison you.

Practice forgiveness and gratitude. Do it daily. Make a conscious effort to forgive all the people in your life who have hurt you. Do it in pieces if you have to. But just do it. People think forgiving is one act. It's an ongoing thing, forever. Just like gratitude, forgiveness is one of the most powerful tools you will ever have. It pulls you out of yourself and gives you traction to push through when you feel like you have nothing. Forgiveness and gratitude are muscles. Exercise them.

Quit dwelling on your age and how old you're going to be when Logan is in high school. Would you rather be a young dad with no tools or an older dad who's present and has some capacity? Mr. Miyagi is just as fierce as Bruce Lee.

Keep leaning forward,

Future John Kim

Your turn.

_____

_____

_____

_____

_____

_____

_____

_____

_____

_____

_____

_____

_____

_____

_____

_____

_____

_____

_____

_____

_____

_____

TODAY'S LISTEN

The Angry Therapist podcast episode titled "A Letter to My Future Self."

DAY TWENTY-SIX

I will no longer live in dread, worry, guilt, shame, or any other low frequency. Today I will do whatever it takes to live on a higher frequency.

TODAY'S MANTRA

TODAY'S ONE THING

Live at a higher frequency. Quantum physics explains that there is nothing inside an atom except energy waves. Atoms continually give off and absorb light and energy, and each has its own distinct frequency or vibration.

For most of my life I lived in worry and dread. I was worried about tomorrow and dreaded today. Living like that put me in a powerless state. It gave me a deeply furrowed brow and heavy, chipped shoulders. It grayed me out. I was merely existing, not truly living. It wasn't until I intentionally stopped swimming in my own shit and started living on a higher frequency that my life finally changed. Most of us default to a lower frequency. It takes a daily effort to change our state.

Think about an average day in your life, from the time you get up to when you go to sleep. Think about what you're doing and who you're around. Check what frequencies you live on.

❏ Love   ❏ Jealousy

❏ Gratitude   ❏ Dread

❏ Hope   ❏ Worry

❏ Creativity   ❏ Pessimism

❏ Optimism   ❏ Shame

❏ Joy   ❏ Hate

Looking at all the lower frequencies you checked, what's one thing you can do to turn each of them into a higher frequency? Remember, these shifts don't need to be big. They don't need to take all day or cost a lot of money. Go back to the basics: focus on simple habits or rituals you can thread into your life when you're feeling out of alignment.

_____

_____

_____

_____

_____

_____

For example, during my many singlehood journeys, I did these things to pull myself out of lower frequencies.

- Motorcycle rides
- A doughnut
- A meaningful conversation with a friend
- Fitness classes
- Walks listening to podcasts
- The beach
- A hard nap
- Journaling
- Etcetera

FUCK IT FRIDAY #TREAT

It's okay if it's not Friday. Give yourself one "fuck it" treat. One thing you don't normally allow yourself to eat because it's "bad," but today, fuck it. You work hard and you deserve this. Whatever you ate, stamp the mess on your fingers in the box below.

DAY TWENTY-SEVEN

There is good in my life. Today I will find it.

TODAY'S ONE THING

Seek the positive. I have a running joke that if my mom won the lottery the first thing she would say is, "Fuck, the taxes I have to pay on this $200 million!" She is not selfish. My mom is actually a very selfless person. But she's wired to see the negative. Always. This comes from her difficult upbringing and her mind/body being locked in survival mode. Constantly scanning for danger (the negative) is what protects us. But if we don't rewire ourselves to start seeing the positive in our lives, we will create our own prison.

It's something I started working on after my divorce. I still struggle with it. I have to consciously remind myself daily to take a deep breath and notice all the good in my life. Or I tend to default to scanning for the negative. My good goggles fall off. I have to put them back on and make a daily intention to catch the negative scanning before those thoughts spread. Like a virus.

Seeking the positive requires training.

POSITIVE EVENTS THIS WEEK

Monday

_____

_____

Tuesday

_____

_____

Wednesday

_____

_____

Thursday

_____

_____

Friday

_____

_____

Saturday

_____

_____

Sunday

_____

_____

TODAY'S VISUALIZATION/ MEDITATION

I've done this often during all my singlehood journeys and still do. Sit or lie down. Pop in earbuds and play Tez Cadey's "Oregon." For the duration of this instrumental song, close your eyes and see all the positive things in your life right now. As the song builds, imagine and step into the experiences and things and relationships you want. Walk into the vision. Feel it in your bones.

DAY TWENTY-EIGHT

I have a vision and plan for my life. Even if it's not concrete, it's alive and forming, and I will continue to feed it.

TODAY'S MANTRA

TODAY'S ONE THING

The 30,000-foot view (aka three-year plan): Imagine a vision board, but using words instead of pictures. Take a beat and see where you are three years from now. What do you want for yourself? Who's around you? What does it feel like in your body? Then write what you see. Write what you feel. Don't overthink it, or cast doubt on what's possible. Just write what you see and feel. It doesn't have to make sense. Don't be modest. Be honest.

I'll go first.

A vacation home in the mountains where I can write. A shipping container turned into a work studio. On the roof, a hammock facing a 360-degree sunset. Dirt bikes. A nonprofit. A farmers' market strawberry. A Netflix special. The Grand Canyon. Zion. Adventures. More books. Fall in New York. Logan on my shoulders picking McIntosh apples. A gathering of close friends and family in Carpinteria. With a spirit-filled breeze. Live music. A celebration of love. Ours, it's a wedding. Unpostured. Vegetables from a garden. Dinner parties with new friends. Podcasting in a real studio. Deep breaths, coming naturally now. Not prescribed. A vintage truck. Pancakes on Sundays. A manual nineties Porsche 911 convertible shooting up the Pacific Coast Highway. Vanessa's blond locks smacking her smiling face. I see our story in her trusting green eyes. She's back in school, getting a PhD. A Spanish-style home surrounded by dancing palm trees, the kind you see in *Dwell* magazine. A crystal sky-blue pool. A breeze on my back, taking me back to when that was all I had. A simple meaningful life. Openness. Flow states. Connection. A marquee, "The Angry Therapist Presents." Shattered. The sound of a motorcycle. Pull back, it's a television show. Unscripted.

Don't think. Just splatter paint with words.

DAILY SWEAT

Run like Forrest Gump. Go at your own pace and distance. But go at least one mile. During the run, play the vision you have for yourself. Don't see it like a movie. Walk into it like it's already happening and you're just experiencing your days. Run. Toward. It.

DAY TWENTY-NINE

Instead of thinking about another relationship, my focus is to build a better relationship with myself first.

TODAY'S
MANTRA

TODAY'S ONE THING

The relationship-with-self agreement. We have agreements for all our transactions and investments. Why not one for the relationship we have with ourselves? Because it all starts or ends here. Review this relationship-with-self agreement. Then take a red pen and mark it up. What would you add, tweak, change?

THE RELATIONSHIP-WITH-SELF AGREEMENT

A. PARTIES.

These amended and related relationship laws are made and entered into on the date of _____ by me and myself. The relationship's purpose shall be to develop and maintain and promote the growth of self. To create the space that supports and champions my story, without needing or depending on someone else to create that space.

B. INTENTIONS.

My intentions in entering this agreement with myself are as follows: To love myself fully, without doubt or hesitation. "Fully" shall be defined as loving with honesty and integrity, pulling from my heart in good faith and seeking the best life for myself. To love, not hate. I agree to execute love to the best of my ability wherever I'm at in my life, with the intention to build something real and lasting.

"Real and lasting" shall be defined as an honest love with healthy intentions and healthy boundaries with others.

C. ACTIONS.

1. Inner Self.

I will do my best to love myself without the residue of the past. "Do my best" will be determined by me according to where I am in my mental/emotional space and inner journey. This may fluctuate depending on external life forces and events. Loving without my past shall include but is not limited to: Not comparing the old me and who I was to the new me and who I am now. Being aware of old self-love patterns, in both thought and behavior, that are unhealthy. Taking action to change these patterns. Not putting pressure or expectations on myself to be or to behave in a way that is not honest to me.

a. Communication.

I agree to try to understand myself with compassion. Not judgment. I will actually listen to myself and acknowledge my needs instead of ignoring or minimizing them. I agree to install a "speed bump" before I say stupid and damning shit to myself.

I agree to express my feelings instead of holding them in, whether from fear or out of habit. I understand the importance of expressing myself, that it's the difference between loving myself and leaving myself.

b. *Ownership.*

I shall make an effort to own what is mine to own. This includes out-of-control emotions and self-sabotaging actions. This includes words and actions that contribute to conflict in my relationship with myself. Also, past events that have wired me in a certain way that may contribute to unhealthy relationship dynamics and patterns. I agree to own triggers as well as negative energy. I agree to process and rewire myself.

2. External Self.

I agree to work on my relationship with my body. With both diet and exercise. Not just for the aesthetics but to feel good and connected to self. I understand that my connection to and relationship with my body is my own responsibility and something I will work on forever, *not* just while I'm single.

I agree to practice self-care. This shall include my mental, emotional, and physical health. I understand that self-care is not "extra" or only executed when life is good. Self-care is mandatory and my responsibility. Mental and emotional self-care may include but is not limited to therapy, self-help books, life coaching, meditation, and spiritual practices. Physical self-care includes and is not limited to daily exercise, a healthy diet, and good hygiene.

a. *Work.*

I shall put in hard work and do everything in my power to pursue my passions and dreams. "Hard work" shall be defined by me and only me. If I'm unemployed or experiencing a life transition, a three-month maximum "getting back on my feet" period shall be granted with no bitching or going into victim mode. During this time, I will make an honest effort to get back on my feet. Parenting a child will also be included in "hard work." Video games will not be allowed.

Sixteen-hour workdays will not be permitted, unless I agree that this work pace is needed—temporarily—to better my quality of life and meet my goals.

Complaining, whining, and excuses shall not be tolerated.

b. *Date Myself Night.*

I agree to put an honest effort into spending alone time with myself, as if I'm doing things with a partner. Activities may vary. There shall be no minimum or maximum number of days or amounts of money required. Date Myself Night shall require my best effort to feel good about myself and splurge on myself.

NO TOLERANCE CLAUSE

Mental or emotional abuse of myself and character assassination of myself shall *not* be tolerated under any circumstances. If spotted, I shall prioritize working through it until it ceases.

LOVE HARD CLAUSE

I shall love myself hard. "Loving hard" shall be defined as making an honest effort to love myself with everything I've got. To not lose myself in any other relationship. To show myself in an authentic way. To be vulnerable. To have healthy boundaries. To communicate and express feelings. To explore and expand my dreams and goals and passions. To be kind to myself and love with an open heart. To forgive myself often. To always be curious about myself instead of judgmental. To believe and be the magic that is me.

"Magic" cannot be defined.

Dated and signed,

_____

I will accept my whole story instead of ripping out chapters.

TODAY'S MANTRA

TODAY'S ONE THING

Write your story as if it's a movie trailer. This is different from the previous visualization exercise, where you walked into your story. It's important to have distance in this version. You are in the audience watching your story like it's playing on the big screen. All the important events that made you who you are today need to be included. You can start wherever you want. Your movie trailer story can be nonlinear. Start now, bookmark it, and come back to this very scene—you in the audience, watching your story. Come full circle. However you see your story playing, take a seat, with some popcorn in your lap, and then take a breath. Hit Play.

MY STORY

Act 1.

_____

_____

_____

_____

_____

_____

_____

_____

_____

_____

Act 2.

_____

_____

_____

_____

_____

_____

_____

_____

Act 3.

_____

_____

_____

_____

_____

_____

_____

_____

_____

TODAY'S JOURNALING

What came up for you as you "played" and wrote your story? Any revelations? How did it feel watching it? Were there chapters you wanted to rip out? Or did you embrace them, maybe for the first time in your life? Did you hear your fight song as you saw yourself getting up or pushing through after hardship, a broken heart, or some other turbulence? Did you find yourself rooting for yourself?

REMINDER: What you've been through, all the events and relationships in your life, were catalysts to your growth and evolution. If they hadn't happened, there would be no story. Many people hate their story and want to rip out chapters they see as full of guilt and shame. Accepting, embracing, and eventually sharing your story is what makes your story greater than you. Remember, all parts of your story have gone into making you *you*. So accept, embrace, and share your story. Because your story is the most valuable thing you will ever own.

_____

_____

_____

_____

_____

_____

_____

TODAY'S LISTEN

This is an important listen. It's not just a song. It's an anthem. For you. I want to end on an emotional note. Play "I Found You" by Alabama Shakes, and as you play it, think about how you found yourself. All the shit you had to go through. To get to this plane in your life and inner journey. To return to the village. Changed. Connected. To. You.

DAY THIRTY-ONE

Congratulations! You finished thirty-one days of being single on purpose. You started each day with a mantra. You did one thing that contributed to building a better relationship with yourself. You sweated, you visualized, you meditated, you dropped into your body. You created new definitions and tried on different mindsets. Hopefully you've had many revelations and shifts in perspective.

But most importantly, you laid tracks. New ones. So these thirty-one days weren't just a onetime thing. They've given you a template, a daily structure to thread into your everyday life. If not all of it, then whatever worked for you.

There is no beginning and end to building a better relationship with yourself. It is a lifestyle, never ending, not something you do just for thirty-one days. I hope this workbook has given you a runway, handrails, and momentum.

Welcome to the first day of the new you.

JOHN KIM

NOTE TO SELF

These three pages are for you. Fill them up. Any notes you want to write for yourself to look back and read when you have hard days. Here, I'll start you off.

Stay off the dating apps until you are ready. And when you're ready, use it as a tool not a means. There is no rush. Be picky and show up authentically. Only use when you feel good about yourself. Not when you're feeling desperate and lonely.

_____

_____

_____

_____

_____

_____

_____

_____

_____

_____

_____

_____

_____

KEEP IN TOUCH

Let me know how you're doing.
theangrytherapist@gmail.com

TEXT ME

Get my daily texts and live Zoom links to monthly gathers so you can do your singlehood journey with like-minded people. Also get mindsets, articles, tools, all texted to you, so you have me in your pocket.

www.theangrytherapist.com